Songs for the Church Choir and Music Group

Book 1

A collection of attractive pieces
compiled by Kevin Mayhew

We hope you enjoy the music in this book. Further copies are available from your local music shop or Christian bookshop.

In case of difficulty, please contact the publisher direct by writing to:

The Sales Department
KEVIN MAYHEW LTD
Rattlesden
Bury St Edmunds
Suffolk
IP30 0SZ

Phone 01449 737978
Fax 01449 737834

Please ask for our complete catalogue of outstanding Church Music.

First published in Great Britain in 1997 by Kevin Mayhew Ltd.

ISBN 1 84003 002 X
ISMN M 57004 064 3
Catalogue No: 1450076

0 1 2 3 4 5 6 7 8 9

Front Cover: *The Ascension – Predella* (detail)
by Benvenuto di Giovanni Guasta. Volterra Pinacoteca.
Courtesy of SuperStock Ltd. Used by permission.
Cover design by Jaquetta Sergeant.

Music Editor: Alistair McPherson

Printed and bound in Great Britain

Contents

Foreword

I have chosen the songs and anthems in this collection for their tunefulness and accessibility. They are the kind of thing that long experience as a church musician and publisher has taught me people like to sing: good tunes, pleasing harmonies and texts that bear witness to the abundant grace and unconditional love of God.

They can be performed in a variety of ways by either a traditional choir or by a music group – or, better still, by both working together.

Most may be sung in unison, with organ accompaniment, though many have optional second parts or descants which may be taken by voice or instrument.

Much that is here is for the choir or music group to sing alone as their contribution to the service. Some pieces can include an element of congregational involvement when desired by way of their refrain. Two (*Praise our God* and *Praise to the Lord*) are written as a dialogue between soloist, congregation and choir, and sound very effective when performed in this way.

Where suitable there are guitar chords, but all the compositions may be accompanied by the sort of unspecified instrumental groups that come together for music making in church. The optional vocal descants and second parts, for example, can just as well be taken by a flute, violin or recorder. Lower parts, suitably transposed, will sound well on clarinet, while any bass instrument will simply work in with the left hand of the keyboard. Because every music group has a different instrumental line-up and musical ability, music directors will wish to make their own decisions about these matters.

I have used all the compositions in this book and they have worked for me. I hope they will help others to 'speak to one another in the words of psalms, hymns and sacred songs' and 'sing hymns to the Lord, with praise in your hearts' (Ephesians 5:19).

KEVIN MAYHEW

For the Saint Edmund's Young People's Choir

O ETERNAL GOD

Text: Jeremy Taylor (1613-1667)
Music: Kevin Mayhew

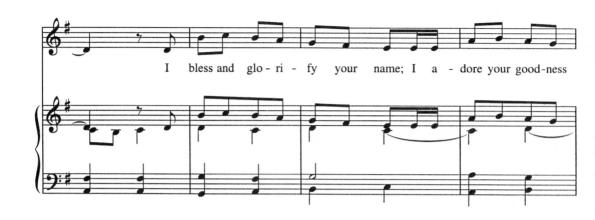

I bless and glo - ri - fy your name; I a - dore your good-ness

and de - light in your love. Take from me ev - 'ry

cresc.

ten - den - cy to - ward sin or va - ni - ty; let my de - sires soar

cresc.

up - wards to your love, that I may hun - ger and

thirst for the bread of life and the wine of

heav'n, and know no love but yours.

7

SONG FOR A YOUNG PROPHET

Text (based on Jeremiah 1) and Music: Damian Lundy
Arranged by Malcolm Archer

Last time

rall.

mind.

D   D   (D7)   G   Em

1. Be - fore I formed you in womb I knew you through and through, I chose you to be mine. Be-

F#m(A)   D   Em   A7   D

D.S.

fore you left your mo-ther's side I called to you, my child, to be my sign.

D.S.

G   Em   F#m(A) D   Em   A7

2. I know that you are very young,
   but I will make you strong;
   I'll fill you up with my word;
   and you will travel though the land,
   fulfilling my command
   which you have heard.

3. And ev'rywhere you are to go
   my hand will follow you;
   you will not be alone.
   In all the danger that you fear
   you'll find me very near,
   your word's my own.

4. With all my strength you will be filled;
   you will destroy and build,
   for that is my design.
   You will create and overthrow,
   reap harvests I will sow;
   you word is mine.

9

WAKE UP, O PEOPLE

Text and Music: Marie Lydia Pereira
Arranged by Christopher Tambling

Wake up, O peo-ple, the

Lord is ve-ry near! Wake up, and stand for the Lord.

Wake up, O peo-ple, the Lord is ve-ry near! Wake up, and stand for the

2. The night of sin has passed. Wake up!
   The light is near at last. Wake up!
   The day star, Christ, the Son of God, will soon appear.

3. To live in love and peace. Wake up!
   To let all quarrels cease. Wake up!
   To live that all you do may stand the light of day.

4. That Christ may be your shield. Wake up!
   That death to life may yield. Wake up!
   That heaven's gate be opened wide again for you.

For Barry Rose and the choristers of St Albans Abbey

WHEN I SURVEY THE WONDROUS CROSS

Text: Isaac Watts
Music: Malcolm Archer

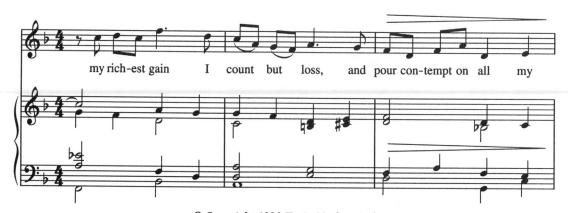

© Copyright 1990 Kevin Mayhew Ltd.
It is illegal to photocopy music.

pride.

All *mf*

2. For-bid it, Lord,   that

I   should   boast,   save   in   the   cross   of   Christ,   my   God:

all the vain things   that   charm   me   most,   I   sac- ri -fice them to   his

blood.

p

3. See from his head,   his

hands, his feet, sor - row and love flow ming - ling down:

did e'er such love and sor - row meet, or thorns com-pose so rich a

did e'er such love and sor - row meet, or thorns com-pose so rich a

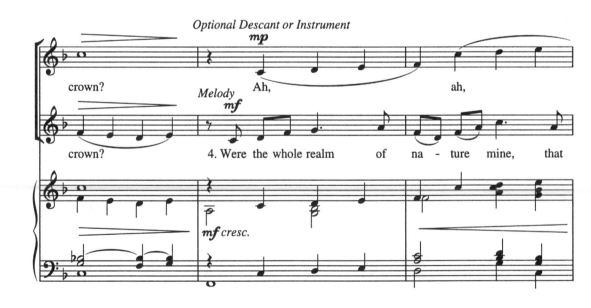

crown?

crown?

Optional Descant or Instrument

Ah, ah,

Melody

4. Were the whole realm of na - ture mine, that

were an off-'ring far too small; love so a-maz - ing,

so di - vine, de-mands my soul, my life, my all.

A - men, A - men.

A - men, A - men.

ah.

LET LOVE BE REAL

Text: Michael Forster
Music: Christopher Tambling

ten - ding,   where ev - 'ry weak - ness may be safe - ly known.   Give me your
liv - ing,   and makes us brave   to be what we might be.   Give me your
plete - ness,   and share the joy   of learn - ing to be whole.   Give me your

C   Cm   G   D7   G   G7

hand,   a - long the de - sert path - way,   give me your love   wher - e - ver we may
strength when   all my words are weak - ness,   give me your love   in spite of all you
hope, through dreams and dis - ap - point - ments,   give me your trust   when all my fail - ings

C   D7   G   Em   Am

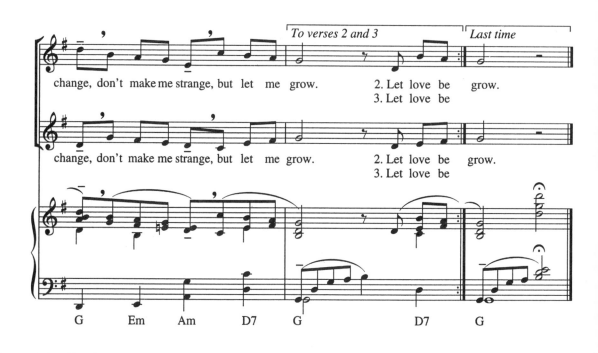

LET OUR PRAISE TO YOU

Text: Bryan Spinks (based on Psalm 141)
Music: Malcolm Archer

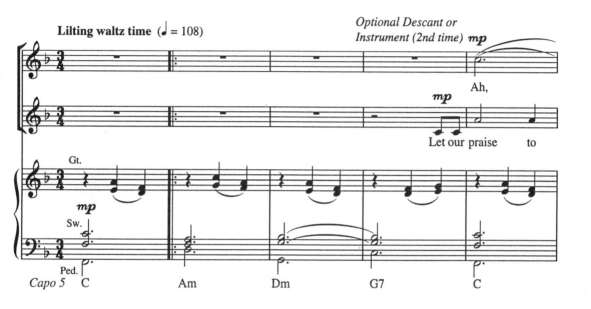

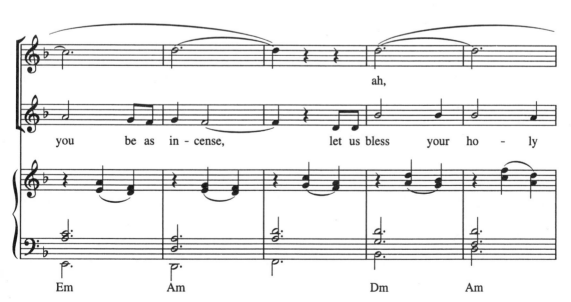

PRAISE OUR GOD

Text: Hubert J. Richards
Music: Andrew Moore

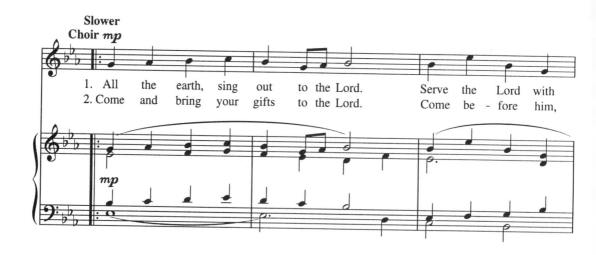

Slower
Choir *mp*

1. All the earth, sing out to the Lord. Serve the Lord with
2. Come and bring your gifts to the Lord. Come be - fore him,

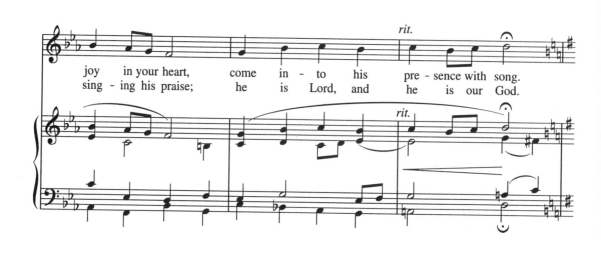

joy in your heart, come in - to his pre - sence with song.
sing - ing his praise; he is Lord, and he is our God.

rit.

Tempo I
Solo *f*

Choir and Congregation

Al - le - lu - ia, al - le - lu - ia. Al - le - lu - ia, al - le - lu - ia.

f

24

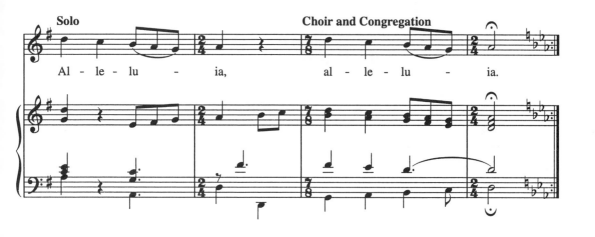

Al - le - lu - ia, al - le - lu - ia.

Slower
Choir *mp*

3. God is good, his love ne -ver ends; he is al - ways

true to his word, he is faith - ful, age u -pon age.

poco rall. *D.S. al Fine*

ON EAGLES' WINGS

Text and Music: Michael Joncas
Arranged by Christopher Tambling

1. You who dwell in the shel-ter of the Lord, who a-bide in his sha-dow for life,

say to the Lord: 'My ref-uge, my rock in whom I trust!'

And he will raise you up on ea-gles' wings, bear you on the

breath of dawn, make you to shine like the sun, and hold you in the

A7   D   (D7)   G   (Em) A7 Bm(D) F#m(A)

Second time to ⊕

palm of his hand.   2. The snare of the fow-ler will

Em   D   F#m(A)   Bm(D) G

ne-ver cap-ture you, and fa-mine will bring you no fear.

F#m(A)   Bm(D) G   D

Un-der his wings your ref - uge, his faith-ful-ness your shield.

F(Dm)   Dm   Gm(B♭)   A7sus4

hand.

3. You need not fear the ter-ror of the night, nor the

D   F♯m(A)   Bm(D) G   F♯m(A)   Bm(D)

ar-row that flies by day; though thou-sands fall a-bout you,

G   D   F(Dm)   Dm

Refrain

near you it shall not come. And he will raise you up on ea-gles' wings,

Gm(B♭)   A7sus4   A7   D

bear you on the breath of dawn, make you to shine like the sun, and

Em   A7   D   (D7)   G   (Em) A7

Last time to Coda

hold you in the palm of his hand. 4. For to his an-gels he's

Bm(D) F#m(A) Em   D   F#m(A) Bm(D) G

giv-en a com-mand to guard you in all of your ways; up - on their hands they will

F#m(A)   Bm(D) G   D   F(Dm)

D.S. al Coda **CODA**

bear you up, lest you dash your foot a-gainst a stone.   and

Dm   Gm(Bb)   A7sus4   F#m(A)

hold you,   hold you in the palm   of his hand.

Bm(D) F#m(A) Em   D   A7   D

Ped. _____

29

PIE JESU

Text: from the Requiem Mass
Music: Gabriel Fauré
Arranged by Alan Ridout

Translation: Holy Lord Jesus, give them everlasting rest.

na e - is, Do - mi-ne, do - na e - is re - qui-em,

na e - is, Do - mi-ne, do - na e - is re - qui-em,

sem - pi - ter - nam re - qui-em, sem - pi - ter - nam

sem - pi - ter - nam re - qui-em, sem - pi - ter - nam

re - qui-em, sem - pi - ter - nam re - qui-em.

re - qui-em, sem - pi - ter - nam re - qui-em.

THE CUP OF BLESSING

Text: Psalm 116
Music: Malcolm Archer

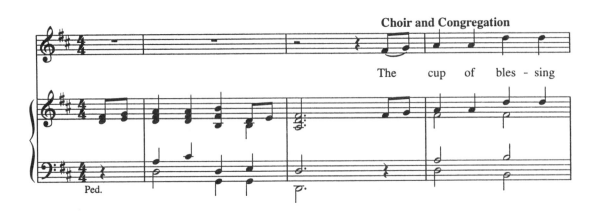

The cup of bles - sing

which we bless, is it not a shar - ing of the blood of Christ?

1. How shall I re - pay the Lord for all his be-ne-fits for me?

I will take the cup of sal-va-tion and call up-on the name of the

Lord. The cup of bless-ing which we bless, is it not a shar-ing

of the blood of Christ? 2. I will pay my vows to the Lord in the

pre-sence of all his peo-ple. Grie-vous in the sight of the Lord is the

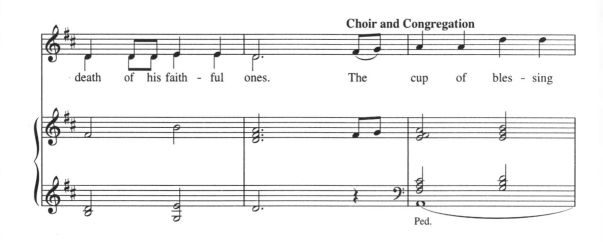

Choir and Congregation

death of his faith - ful ones. The cup of bles - sing

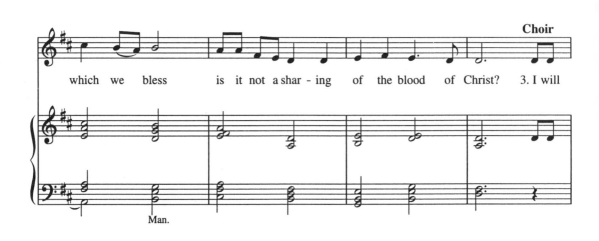

Choir

which we bless is it not a shar - ing of the blood of Christ? 3. I will

Man.

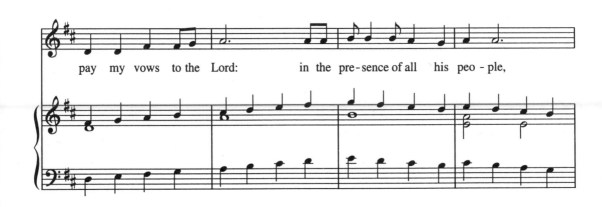

pay my vows to the Lord: in the pre - sence of all his peo - ple,

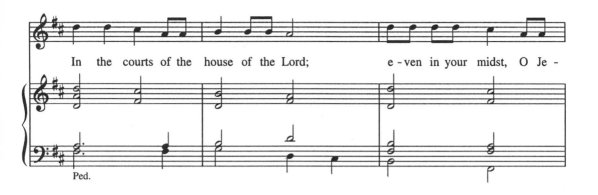

In the courts of the house of the Lord; e - ven in your midst, O Je -

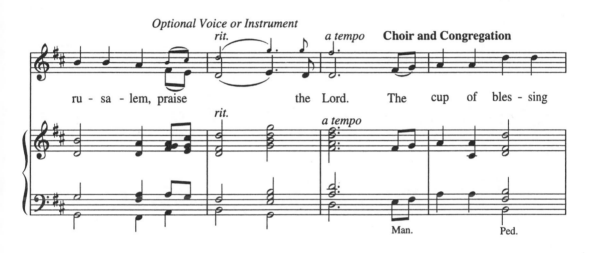

Optional Voice or Instrument

rit. *a tempo* **Choir and Congregation**

rit. *a tempo*

ru - sa - lem, praise the Lord. The cup of bles - sing

Man. Ped.

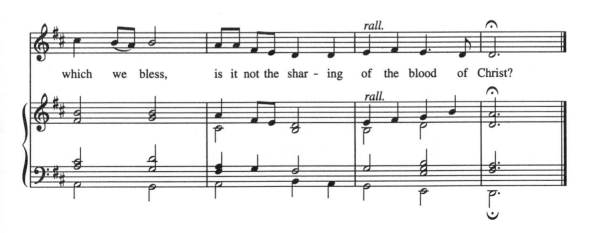

rall.

which we bless, is it not the shar - ing of the blood of Christ?

rall.

For Jessie, with love

MAGNIFICAT

Text: Michael Forster
Music: Kevin Mayhew

shar-ing in the song of Ma - ry,

G (G7) C D G - Am -

Refrain

filled with un - ex - pec - ted grace. Mag-ni - fi - cat, mag -

B(B7) Em A7 D

ni - fi-cat, praise the Lord, my soul; mag-ni - fi-cat, mag -

G Em A7 D

To verses *D.C.* *Last time*

ni - fi-cat, praise the Lord, my soul. praise the Lord, my soul.

G Em A7 D Em A7 D

2. God has rocked the earth's foundations,
   turned its values upside-down:
   strength is overcome by weakness
   and the humble wear the crown.
   Now the pow'r of God in action
   undermines the nations' pride,
   lifts the poor and feeds the hungry,
   pushing rich and proud aside.

3. Join the song of praise and protest
   as the voiceless find a voice,
   as the pow'rless rise triumphant
   and the broken hearts rejoice.
   Now the God of all creation
   rights the long-accepted wrongs;
   let the voices of the nations
   swell the liberation song.

LISTEN

Text and Music: Aniceto Nazareth
Arranged by Malcolm Archer

Lis - ten, let your heart keep seek - ing; lis - ten to his con - stant speak - ing;

lis - ten to the Spi - rit call - ing you.

Lis - ten to his in - spi - ra - tion; lis - ten to his in - vi - ta - tion;

lis - ten to the Spi - rit call - ing you.

C   Am   Em

mf cresc.

1. He's in the sound of the thun - der, in the whis - per of the breeze.
2. He's in the laugh - ter of child - ren, in the pat - ter of the rain.
3. He's in the noise of the ci - ty, in the sing - ing of the birds.

legato

mf cresc.

Ped.
C   D   Bm(D)   Em   Am   D7   G   (G7)

mf cresc.   *dim.*   D.S.

He's in the might of the whirl- wind, in the roar - ing of the seas.
Hear him in cries of the suff- 'ring, in their moan -ing and their pain.
And in the night -time, the still- ness helps you lis - ten to his word.

D.S.

mf cresc.

dim.

C   D   Bm(D)   Em   Am   D7   B7sus4 B7

CODA Solo soprano

pp   *rall.*

Lis - ten to the Spi - rit call - ing you.

rall.

pp

Ped.
D   Bm(D)   A7   F(Dm)   Em

41

For my mother

A CELTIC BLESSING

Text: Traditional Gaelic
Music: Martin Setchell

fields. And un - til we meet a - gain, may God

hold you in the palm of his hand.

Solo Flute

Man.

Sw.

1st Voice *mp*

2. May the road rise up to meet you,

2nd Voice or Instrument *mp*

2. May the road rise up to meet you,

mp

Ped.

BEHOLD, THE LORD WILL COME!

Text: Michael Forster
Music: Colin Mawby

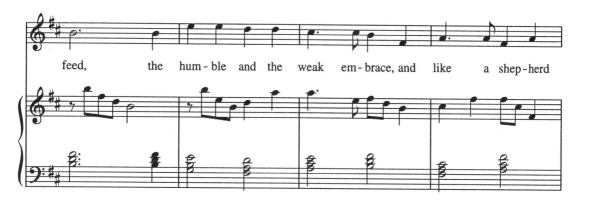

feed, the hum-ble and the weak em-brace, and like a shep-herd

lead. All things shall come to light, 'though hi-ther-to con-

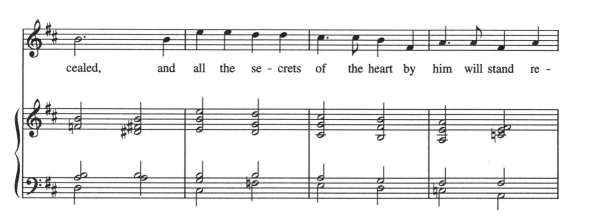

cealed, and all the se-crets of the heart by him will stand re-

Optional Descant or Instrument

What joy-ous task is ours, to he-rald and ac-claim the

vealed. What joy-ous task is ours, to he-rald and ac-claim the

co-ming of the liv-ing Lord, of high e-ter-nal name, of

co-ming of the liv-ing Lord, of high e-ter-nal name, of

high e-ter-nal name!

high e-ter-nal name!

PRAISE TO THE LORD

Text: Hubert J. Richards (based on Psalm 95)
Music: Richard Lloyd

Bles-sed be God for e-ver, A-men, bles-sed be God for e-ver, A-men,

bles-sed be God for e-ver, A-men.

Choir and Congregation

Bles-sed be God for e-ver, A-men,

bles-sed be God for e-ver, A-men, bles-sed be God for e-ver, A-men.

Choir *mf*

1. Come, sing a new song to the Lord; come, sing to the Lord
3. Let all cre-a-tion shout for joy; come, wor ship the Lord

bles - sed be God   for   e - ver, A - men.

COME TO ME

Text: Delores Dufner, OSB
Music: Rosalie Bonighton

drink the wa - ter I will give. If you knew what gift I
come that I may give you rest. Drink the cup of life I
find re - fresh-ment in this place. If you knew the gift I

D.C.

of - fer, you would come to me and live.
of - fer; at this ta - ble be my guest.
of - fer, you would turn and seek my face.

D.C.

PANIS ANGELICUS

Text: Thomas Aquinas
Music: César Franck
Arranged by Alan Ridout and John Ballantine

Pa - nis an - ge-li-cus   fit   pa - nis ho - mi-num;

Translation: *The bread of angels becomes bread for humans; the bread of heaven is the fulfilment of its foreshadowing. What a wonder! The Lord becomes the food of his poor and lowly servant.*

REJOICE IN THE LORD

Text: Psalm 33: 1-9
Music: Malcolm Archer (b.1952)

ah,

Lord. 3. He ga-ther'd wa-ters of the sea as in a wa-ter-skin and

ah, ah,

laid up the deep in his trea-sures. Let the whole earth fear the

Lord and let all the in-ha-bi-tants of the world stand in

ah,   ah,

awe of him.   For he spoke and it was

ah,   ah,

Choir and Cong.

done: he com - man - ded and it stood fast. The

earth is filled with the lov - ing kind - ness of the Lord.